Teaching Notes

C

In
V
C

MW01123012

Introduction

The Sparrows stories at Stage 3 provide consolidation for children who need plenty of practice before moving to the next stage. The stories are at the same level of difficulty as the other stories at Stage 3. The same key words and high frequency words are used. New nouns and verbs are usually obvious from the illustrations.

Sparrows introduce new characters and new settings, broadening the children's reading base. These stories do not include Biff, Chip and Kipper.

To help children approach each new book in this stage with confidence, prepare the children for reading by talking about the book, asking questions and using the support material to introduce new characters and settings.

As children read these stories they are encouraged to read independently through: using their knowledge of letter sounds; learning to recognise high frequency words on sight; using the pictures and the sense of the story to work out new vocabulary.

How to introduce the books

Before reading the story, always read the title and talk about the picture on the cover. Go through the book together, looking at the pictures and talking about them. If there are context words (listed in the chart on page 4 of this booklet) that are new or unfamiliar, point them out and read them with the children.

Read the story to the children, encouraging confident children to join in with you.

This booklet provides suggestions for using the books in group and independent activities. Prompts and ideas are provided for introducing and reading each book with a child or group of children. Suggestions are also provided for writing, speaking and listening and cross-curricular links. You can use these suggestions to follow on from your reading, or use at another time.

Take-Home Cards are also available for each book. These provide friendly prompts and suggestions for parents reading with their children. You can store the relevant card with each book in your "Take-Home" selection of titles.

Reading skills

Stage 3 develops:
- the ability to predict meaning through the continual support of strong picture-cueing and familiar contexts
- the ability to locate and use a growing bank of familiar words, letters and letter sounds
- an awareness of a broader range of settings
- confidence in writing sentences and simple stories.

Vocabulary chart

Midge in Hospital	**Reception High frequency words** a at go mum she see the they to was
	Years 1 to 2 High frequency words bad be came gave good him his home in man not off so took want
	Context words ambulance bike books didn't doctor fell foot friends frightened fruit hospital it's looked nan sweet toy
Roy and the Budgie	**Reception High frequency words** a at away for get he in it my no said the they to was went
	Years 1 to 2 High frequency words an called had saw see
	Context words budgie couldn't flew it's looked oh ostrich outside thanks wood zoo-keeper
Pip at the Zoo	**Reception High frequency words** a dad no said the to was went you
	Years 1 to 2 High frequency words do gave her over some took want water
	Context words bananas crocodiles deer elephants feed finger food fruit hat helped monkeys parrots pecked pushed sweets thanks zoo zoo-keeper
Joe and the Bike	**Reception High frequency words** a come dad he in it on no said the to was went
	Years 1 to 2 High frequency words fell gave him his off what
	Context words bike birthday front liked oh pushed race rider shouted speedway
Midge and the Eggs	**Reception High frequency words** a at and come go he I in mum my no play said the went
	Years 1 to 2 High frequency words about can't down got had his put man more saw some these wanted wants
	Context words bag basket cart eggs forgot friend(s) go-kart looked oh shop sorry
Pip and the Little Monkey	**Reception High frequency words** a and at dad it mum the they to was
	Years 1 to 2 High frequency words got her home house little ran too took with
	Context words better cried happy helped ill its jumped keep looked monkey played wanted zoo zoo-keeper

Curriculum coverage chart

	Speaking and listening	Reading	Writing
Midge in Hospital			
NLS/NC	1f, 2d, 8c	W9, S1, T2	S8
Scotland	Level B	Level B	Level B
N. Ireland	Activities: c, f, g Outcomes: b, c, d, g	Activities: b, c, f Outcomes: b, d, e	Outcomes: a, c, e, f
Wales	Range: 2, 5, 6 Skill: 1, 2, 5	Range: 5, 6 Skill: 1, 2	Range: 3, 4, 6 Skill: 1, 4, 8, 9
Roy and the Budgie			
NLS/NC	1a, 2a, 3a, 8c	W10, S9, T2, T5	T8
Scotland	Level B	Level B	Level B
N. Ireland	Activities: e, i Outcomes: a, c, e	Activities: a, e, f Outcomes: b, i	Outcomes: a, f, h, i
Wales	Range: 1, 3 Skill: 2, 4, 5	Range: 4, 5, 6 Skill: 1, 2	Range: 2, 3, 4, 7 Skill: 5, 6, 8, 9
Pip at the Zoo			
NLS/NC	1d, 2c, 3e	W3, W4, S5, T2, T7	T11
Scotland	Level B	Level B	Level B
N. Ireland	Activities: e, i Outcomes: a, c, e	Activities: c, f, h Outcomes: c, j	Outcomes: a, b, f, i
Wales	Range: 1, 3 Skill: 2, 4, 5	Range: 4, 5, 6 Skill: 1, 2	Range: 1, 3, 4, 7 Skill: 5, 6, 8
Joe and the Bike			
NLS/NC	1c, 3d, 9a	W1, W9, W10, S3, T15	T14
Scotland	Level B	Level B	Level B
N. Ireland	Activities: c, e, g Outcomes: b, d, g	Activities: f, g, h Outcomes: d, e, j	Outcomes: b, c, h, i
Wales	Range: 1, 2, 5 Skill: 1, 2, 3	Range: 2, 4 Skill: 1, 2	Range: 3, 4 Skill: 1, 5, 7, 8
Midge and the Eggs			
NLS/NC	1d, 2a, 10b	W3, W7, S3, T5	W6
Scotland	Level B	Level B	Level B
N. Ireland	Activities: e, i Outcomes: a, c, e	Activities: f, h Outcomes: c, g, k	Outcomes: a, b, c
Wales	Range: 1, 3 Skill: 2, 4, 5	Range: 2, 5, 6 Skill: 1, 2	Range: 1, 4, 6 Skill: 1, 7, 8
Pip and the Little Monkey			
NLS/NC	1e, 2b, 3b	W5, S2, S6, T2, T4	W8
Scotland	Level B	Level B	Level B
N. Ireland	Activities: c, e, g Outcomes: b, d, g	Activities: c, e Outcomes: b, c, h, d	Outcomes: c, h, i
Wales	Range: 1, 2, 5 Skill: 1, 2, 3	Range: 2, 6 Skill: 1,2	Range: 4, 5, 7 Skill: 2, 5, 7

Midge in Hospital

Before reading

- Look at the front cover and read the title. Ask the children to predict how Midge ends up in hospital.
- Turn to page 1 and confirm the children's predictions.

During reading

- Ask the children to read the story. Praise the children for reading the high frequency words on sight.
- Encourage them to use the pictures to help them read new words (e.g. page 3 "ambulance", page 7 "doctor", page 9 "toy", page 11 "fruit", page 13 "books").

Observing Check that the children:

- use graphic knowledge to work out, predict and check the meanings of unfamiliar words (Y1T1 T2)
- read on sight approximately 30 high frequency words (Y1T1 W9).

Group and independent reading activities

Text level work

Objective To use phonological, contextual, grammatical and graphic knowledge to work out, predict and check the meanings of unfamiliar words (Y1T1 T2).

- Turn to page 3. Ask the children: *How did you work out the word "ambulance"?* Encourage the children to share their ideas if they differ from each other's.
- Ask them to look through the book and find other words that were difficult to work out. Ask: *Did you have to use the pictures, sentence or letter sounds to work out the word?*

Observing Can the children find examples of when they used different strategies to work out unfamiliar words?

Sentence level work

Objective To expect written text to make sense and to check for sense if it does not (Y1T1 S1).

- On page 3, read the text inaccurately: *The firemen came. The boys look at Midge's fossil.* Discuss with the children what is wrong with what you have just read. Ask: *Does that make sense?*
- Repeat on a further page and ask: *Does that make sense?* Ask: *Is it important for the writing to make sense?*

Observing Can the children hear when text does not make sense?

Word level work

Objective To read on sight approximately 30 high frequency words identified for Y1 and Y2 (Y1T1 W9).

- Ask the children to find these words in the text: "bad", "be", "came", "gave", "good", "him", "his", "home", "in", "man", "not", "off", "so", "took", "want".
- Talk to the children about how these words help us to read and when we see these words we have to read them straight away and not sound out each letter.
- Ask the children to read a sentence to the group and prompt the key word recognition in the sentence. Read the sentence, sounding out the key words, and discuss which method is best.

Observing Can the children recognise and read high frequency words?

Comprehension

Ask the children:

- *How did Midge fall off his bike?* (p1 illustration: rough ground)
- *On page 4, where was Midge being taken?* (X-ray department at St. Mary's Hospital.)
- *On pages 6 and 7, how many doctors helped Midge?* (two)
- *On page 14, why did Midge think that hospital was not so bad?* (Visitors brought him gifts and he had other children to play with.)

Speaking and listening activities

Objectives Take into account the needs of their listeners (1f); listen to others' reactions (2d); describe events and experiences (8c).

● Discuss a time when someone has hurt himself or herself. Talk to the children about what they should do if someone is hurt and encourage them to offer suggestions.

● Ask the children to re-enact stories of such events using either dolls or role-play.

◀▶ **Cross-curricular links**
Geography: How Can We Make Our Local Area Safer?
Music: Feel the Pulse

Writing

Objective To begin using full stops to demarcate sentences (Y1T1 S8).

● Ask the children to write sentences about the people who can help us and what they can help us with, e.g. "The police can help if I am lost." "The doctor can help if I am hurt."

● Remind the children to use a full stop at the end of their sentence.

Roy and the Budgie

Before reading

- Show the cover to the children and ask: *What and who can you see?*
- Introduce the term "budgie" and ask the children to read the title.
- Ask: *What is the budgie's name and what does it do on page 2?*
  Encourage the children to look at pages 1 and 2 to find the answers.

During reading

- Ask the children to read the story. Praise and encourage them while they read and prompt them to self-correct.
- On page 6, check the children use different strategies to work out the unfamiliar word "wood". Ask them to explain its meaning.
- On page 9, check the children use different strategies to work out the unfamiliar word "ostrich". Ask them to explain its meaning.

Observing Check that the children:

- use phonological, contextual, grammatical and graphic knowledge to work out, predict and check the meanings of unfamiliar words and to make sense of what they read (Y1T1 T2).

Group and independent reading activities

Text level work

Objective To describe story settings and incidents and relate them to own experience and that of others (Y1T1 T5).

- Sit in a circle and pass an object round to indicate whose turn it is to speak. Ask each child to say something about the "wood" in the story using his/her own experience.

Observing Can the children relate the story setting to their own experience?

Sentence level work

Objective To use a capital letter for the personal pronoun "I" and for the start of a sentence (Y1T1 S9).

You will need paper in the shape of speech bubbles.
- Ask: *What do you think Roy might be saying on page 4?* (e.g. "I can't reach." "I need longer arms.")
- Ask them to write down what Roy might say. Encourage them to refer to the text for clues.
- Repeat for page 7.

Observing Do the children write a capital letter for the pronoun "I"?

Word level work

Objective To recognise the critical features of words, e.g. length, common spelling patterns and words within words (Y1T1 W10).

- Write the story title on the board. Discuss with the children what the three words, "Roy", "and", "the", have in common? (All have three letters.)
- Encourage the children to look through the text for other three-letter words and to make a list of them.
- Can the children then find words with four, five, and six letters? Ask: *What is the longest word?*

Observing Do the children recognise long and short words on sight or do they count the letters?

Comprehension

Ask the children:
- *How did Joey escape?* (p2 Joey flew out the window.)
- *What was the ostrich's name?* (p9 illustration: Oswald)
- *On page 13, how did Roy know the man was a zoo-keeper?* (illustration: He has "zoo" on his arm and special clothing, e.g. a cap.)
- *How do you think the ostrich escaped from the zoo?* (p16 illustration: A rope tied to his neck broke.)

Speaking and listening activities

Objectives Speak with clear diction and appropriate intonation (1a); sustain concentration (2a); take turns in speaking (3a); describe events and experiences (8c).

- Discuss with the children what happened to Roy at the beginning of the story. (He lost Joey.)
- Encourage the children to share a time when they lost something and ask them to explain how it made them feel.
- Encourage them to listen to each others' stories and to speak audibly so that the others can hear when relating their story.

◀▶ **Cross-curricular links**
Geography: the local area
Music: Taking Off

Writing

Objective Through shared and guided writing to apply phonological, graphic knowledge and sight vocabulary to spell words accurately (Y1T1 T8).

- Remove an object from the classroom. (Ensure it is something that the children are familiar with and see every day.) Tell the children something precious has been lost in the classroom.
- Ask them to write a "Lost" poster for the object to be placed around the school to help find it.
- Encourage the children to use their phonological and graphic knowledge, and sight vocabulary, as they write.

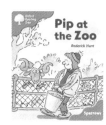

Pip at the Zoo

Before reading

- Read the title. Ask the children: *What is a zoo? What is Pip doing on the front cover? What animals might you see in a zoo?*
- Look through the book and discuss what the animals do to Pip (p7 "pushed", p9 and p11 "took", p13 "pecked"). Ask: *What does Pip think the crocodiles will do to her?* (eat her)

During reading

- Ask the children to read the story.
- Periodically ask the children to say the initial or final phonemes they can hear in a word they have just read. Ensure the children are hearing it and not reading it off the text. (Cover the text while they think of the phoneme.)
- Praise the children who use a variety of strategies to work out unfamiliar words.

Observing Check that the children:

- use phonological, contextual, grammatical and graphic knowledge to work out, predict and check the meanings of unfamiliar words and to make sense of what they read (Y1T1 T2)
- practise and secure the ability to hear initial and final phonemes in CVC words, e.g. fit, mat, pan (Y1T1 W3).

Group and independent reading activities

Text level work

Objective To re-enact stories in a variety of ways, e.g. through role-play, using dolls or puppets (Y1T1 T7).

- Encourage the children to re-enact the story using puppets (or if puppets are not available, through role-play).
- Prompt the children to remember the sequence of events when retelling the story.

Observing Can the children re-enact the story?

Sentence level work

Objective To recognise full stops and capital letters when reading, and name them correctly (Y1T1 S5).

- Ask the children to look carefully at the title. Ask: *How many capital letters can you see?* Discuss why "Pip" and "Zoo" have capital letters.
- Ask: *Is there a full stop in the title?* Encourage the children to give reasons for their answers.
- Look through the story, at both the text and illustrations, and encourage the children to find the capital letters and full stops.

Observing Can the children identify full stops and capital letters?

Word level work

Objective To discriminate and segment all three phonemes in CVC words (Y1T1 W4).

- Ask the children to sound out the three phonemes in the word "hat". Encourage them to list as many words as they can that also only have three phonemes. Point out the words that rhyme.
- Ask the children to think of different words that have the same beginning as "ca" but have a different last letter to "t". (cap, can, car, cab)

Observing Can the children differentiate between sounds and what rhymes and does not rhyme?

Comprehension

Ask the children:
- *On page 6, what is Dad holding and why?* (A first aid kit which Dad used to bandage the deer's leg.)
- *How did the monkey steal Pip's hat?* (p9 illustration: By swinging down from a tree on a rope.)
- *Why did Pip give the elephants some water?* (All animals need to drink to stay alive.)

- *What is Dad doing on page 12?* (mending a perch)
- *Why did Pip not want to help feed the crocodiles?* (She was frightened of being eaten by them.)

Speaking and listening activities

Objectives Focus on the main point(s) (1d); make relevant comments (2c); give reasons for opinions and actions (3e).

- Recap on all the different things that happened to Pip while she was helping her dad.
- Ask the children to give reasons why the animals did all those things to her.
- Discuss what might have happened if Pip had helped her dad feed the crocodiles.

◀▶ Cross-curricular links
D & T: Eat More Fruit and Vegetables
ICT: information around us
PE: dance

Writing

Objective To make simple picture storybooks with sentences, modelling them on basic text conventions, e.g. cover, author's name, title, layout (Y1T1 T11).

- Ask the children to make a book about animals at a zoo. Encourage them to think of all the different things the animals might do. (e.g. "The elephants play in the water." "The monkeys swing on the branches.")
- Encourage them to write a sentence for each animal on each page.

Joe and the Bike

Before reading

- Read the title and ask the children: *What do you think will happen to Joe and his bike?*
- Look through the book to confirm the children's predictions.
- Talk about what is happening on each page, introducing and pointing out the difficult words and phrases (e.g. "speedway", "rider", "in front").

During reading

- Ask the children to read the story. Encourage them as they read and prompt when necessary.
- Praise the children who retained the words you introduced above in "Before reading" and who are able to recognise high frequency words.
- Encourage the children to look closely at the words "shouted", "pushed", "liked" and "rider". Help them to recognise the words within the words.

Observing Check that the children:

- read on sight approximately 30 high frequency words identified for Y1 and Y2 (Y1T1 W9)
- recognise the critical features of words, e.g. length, common spelling patterns and words within words (Y1T1 W10).

Group and independent reading activities

Text level work

Objective To make simple lists for planning, reminding, etc. (Y1T1 T15).

- Ask the children to look in the book and write a list of things that Joe or his dad need to take part in their races.

Observing Can the children write a list?

Sentence level work

Objective To draw on grammatical awareness (Y1T1 S3).

- Talk to the children about how the story happens in the past.
- List the verbs in the story, using the present tense form (e.g. is, shout, says, push, give, like).
- Ask the children to re-write the verbs in the past tense, using the story to help them.

Observing Are the children aware of the difference between the past and present tenses?

Word level work

Objective From YR, to practise and secure the ability to rhyme (Y1T1 W1).

- Ask the children: *I know a word that rhymes with "hike" in this book. Can you find it?*
- Ask the children to find the word and think of other words that rhyme with "bike".
- Repeat with the words: spent, tin, face, bell, had.

Observing Are the children able to hear the rhymes and match the words to rhyming words?

Comprehension

Ask the children:
- *On page 1, who was allowed through the gate?* (Joe)
- *On page 2, what is Joe holding, and who is it for?* (A helmet; his dad's)
- *On page 4, who is in front?* (Joe's dad)
- *On page 7, how is dad feeling?* (surprised, shocked)
- *What time of year is it when Joe is in the race?* (p13 illustration: winter)

Speaking and listening activities

Objectives Organise what they say (1c); extend their ideas in the light of discussion (3d); listen to each other (9a).

- Discuss with the children how Joe was feeling when he fell off his bike. (hurt, angry, mad, embarrassed)
- Ask them to describe an incident when they felt mad and upset at the same time.
- Encourage them to listen to each others' stories.

◀▶ **Cross-curricular links**
D&T: moving pictures
Numeracy: ordinal numbers

Writing

Objective To write captions for their own work (Y1T1 T14).

- Look at the front cover and ask the children to draw a picture of themselves and their favourite toy.
- Prompt them to write a caption: "_____ and the _____."

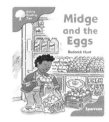

Midge and the Eggs

Before reading

- Look at the front cover and read the title together. Ask the children: *What do you think is going to happen to the eggs?*
- Look at the book to confirm the children's predictions. Ensure the children see the pages on which the eggs actually get broken (pages 9 and 19).

During reading

- Ask the children to read the story. Praise and encourage them for reading with expression and for reading fluently.
- Ensure the children are reading high frequency words matched to their reading group (a, at, and, come, go, he, I, in, mum, my, no, play, said, the, went, about, can't, down, got, had, his, put, man, more, saw, some, these, wanted, wants).
- Prompt the children to read the words on sight and not to use their phonological knowledge to work them out.

Observing Check that the children:

- read with appropriate expression and intonation (Y1T1 S3)
- read on sight high frequency words specific to graded books matched to the abilities of reading groups (Y1T1 W7).

Group and independent reading activities

Text level work

Objective To describe story settings and incidents and relate them to own experience and that of others (Y1T1 T5).

- With the children, recap on all the different places Midge went past on his way back from the shop.
- Ask the children to share any times when they were supposed to be doing something for their mum but were distracted by something or someone.

Observing Are the children able to recall the settings from the story? Can they relate these events to their own experiences?

Sentence level work

Objective To draw on grammatical awareness, to read with appropriate expression and intonation, e.g. in reading to others, or to dolls, puppets (Y1T1 S3).

- Turn to pages 4–5. Encourage a child to read these pages.
- Discuss with the children what kinds of expression could be used to read these pages.
- Ask them to re-read the sentences to each other, using the appropriate expression.

Observing Can the children use and apply appropriate expression when reading the story?

Word level work

Objective From YR to practise and secure the ability to hear initial and final phonemes in CVC words, e.g. fit, mat, pan (Y1T1 W3).

- On page 2, help the children hear the initial and final phonemes in the word "shop". Discuss how "sh" is making one sound and not two sounds.
- On page 3, praise the children for reading "bag" and ask them to tell you the final phoneme in the word.
- Ask the children to find a word in the story that has the final phoneme "g". Repeat for different phonemes featured in the text (e.g. "w", "t", "m").

Observing Can the children identify the final and initial phonemes requested?

Comprehension

Ask the children:
- *What did Midge's mum want the eggs for?* (p1 for a recipe)
- *What else did the egg shop sell?* (p3 yoghurt, milk)
- *On page 19, why did the man pick up Midge's bag?* (He thought it was rubbish and put it in the dustbin lorry.)

- *On page 23, why is the man scratching his head?* (He is wondering why Midge and his mum have come to buy more eggs again.)
- *Look at page 16. Will the eggs get back home in one piece?* (Probably not because they are being thrown on the ground.)

Speaking and listening activities

Objectives Focus on the main point(s) (1d); sustain concentration (2a); share ideas and experiences (10b).

- Discuss with the children what might happen next to the eggs. Go round the group and ask each individual to predict what might happen next.

◀▶ **Cross-curricular links**
Geography: How Can We Make Our Local Area Safer?
ICT: understanding instructions and making things happen
PE: games

Writing

Objective To represent in writing the three phonemes in CVC words, spelling them first in rhyming sets, then in non-rhyming sets (Y1T1 W6).

- Ask the children to write the word "bag". Encourage them to count the number of phonemes in this word.
- Encourage them to draw three short lines in a horizontal row for three missing letters. Give them clues to another three-letter word, e.g. *I am something you wear on your head outside.* (hat or cap)
- Ask the children to write the three phonemes they can hear in this word on their lines. Repeat several times.

Pip and the Little Monkey

Before reading

- Read the title together and ask the children: *Why is Pip looking after the little monkey?* Prompt the children to look through the book to find the answer.
- Talk about what is happening on each page and introduce new or difficult words to the children, e.g. "zoo-keeper", "ill", "home", "better", "cried", "house", "jumped".
- Ask: *How did the monkey get better?*

During reading

- Ask the children to read the story. Encourage the children to read fluently and prompt them to re-read a sentence once they have worked out all the words.
- Praise the children who are demonstrating an awareness of grammar to decipher new and unfamiliar words, e.g. "helped", "ill", "took".
- Periodically ask the children to explain what is happening and encourage them to point to any text they refer to.

Observing Check that the children:

- read familiar, simple stories and poems independently, point while reading and make correspondence between words said and read (Y1T1 T4)
- use awareness of the grammar of a sentence to decipher new or unfamiliar words, e.g. predict text from the grammar, read on, leave a gap and re-read (Y1T1 S2).

Group and independent reading activities

Text level work

Objective To use phonological, contextual, grammatical and graphic knowledge to work out, predict and check the meanings of unfamiliar words and to make sense of what they read (Y1T1 T2).

- Discuss with the children new words used in the text. For example, on page 6, ask: *How did you work out the word "home" at the end of the sentence?* Prompt the children to explain what strategies they used, e.g. the illustrations, the phonics, the sentence structure.
- Encourage the children to show their understanding of what they have read by explaining what has happened and why.

Observing Can the children explain what they have read? Are they using a variety of strategies to work out new and unfamiliar words?

Sentence level work

Objective To begin using the term "sentence" to identify sentences in text (Y1T1 S6).

- Discuss with the children what clues help us to work out if we are reading a sentence. Compare the text inside the book with the blurb on the back cover. Ask: *Which text is written in sentences?*
- Ask: *How many sentences are in this story?* Ensure the children recognise two sentences on page 11.

Observing Can the children identify sentences in the text?

Word level work

Objective To blend phonemes (Y1T1 W5).

- Turn to page 15 and read the sentence with the children. Re-read the word "played" and count the phonemes as you say the word: *pl-ay-ed*.
- Discuss with the children the first two letters "p" and "l" and how they are blended together to make a new sound "pl".
- Turn to page 19 and ask the children to find the two letters at the beginning of the word that are blended together to make one sound. ("cr")

Observing Can the children verbally blend the two letters together to make a new sound?

Comprehension

Ask the children:

- *On page 3, how is Pip helping her dad?* (She is helping her dad wash an elephant.)
- *What house number does Pip live at?* (p7 illustration: number 39)
- *What other animals does Pip like?* (p15 illustration: elephants and giraffes)
- *How did they take the monkey back to the zoo?* (p19 in a cage)
- *On page 16, why was Pip happy?* (p15 Because the monkey was happy.)

Speaking and listening activities

Objectives Include relevant detail (1e); remember specific points that interest them (2b); relate their contributions to what has gone on before (3b).

- Discuss with the children how Pip looked after the monkey.
- Talk about what responsibilities the children have at home and what these involve (e.g. looking after a pet or younger sibling).

◀▶ Cross-curricular links

D&T: homes
PE: dance

Writing

Objective Through shared and guided writing to apply phonological, graphic knowledge and sight vocabulary to spell words accurately (Y1T1 W8).

- Ask the children to write a letter to Pip from the zoo saying, "Thank you for looking after the monkey and making it feel better".

Oxford Reading Tree resources at this level

Stage 3

Teacher support
- Teacher's Handbook
- Flopover Book
- Big Book for Stage 3 Stories
- Guided Reading Cards for Stage 3 Stories
- Take-Home Card for each story
- Extended Stories
- Storytapes / More Storytapes
- Context Cards
- Workbooks 3a and 3b
- Sequencing Cards Photocopy Masters
- Group Activity Sheets Book 1 Stages 1–3
- ORT Games Stages 1–3
- Woodpeckers Introductory Phonic Workbooks A & B

Further reading
- Fireflies Non-Fiction
- Fact Finders Units A and B
- Acorns and More Acorns Poetry

Electronic
- Clip Art
- Stage 3 Talking Stories
- ORT Online www.OxfordReadingTree.com
- Floppy and Friends

For introducing phonics
- First Phonics Stage 3

For developing phonics
- Alphabet frieze, Tabletop Alphabet Mats, Alphabet Photocopy Masters
- Card Games
- First Story Rhymes

OXFORD
UNIVERSITY PRESS

Great Clarendon Street, Oxford OX2 6DP

Oxford University Press is a department of the University of Oxford. It furthers the University's objective of excellence in research, scholarship, and education by publishing worldwide in

Oxford New York

Auckland Cape Town Dar es Salaam Hong Kong Karachi Kuala Lumpur Madrid Melbourne Mexico City Nairobi New Delhi Shanghai Taipei Toronto

With offices in

Argentina Austria Brazil Chile Czech Republic France Greece Guatemala Hungary Italy Japan Poland Portugal Singapore South Korea Switzerland Thailand Turkey Ukraine Vietnam

Oxford is a registered trade mark of Oxford University Press in the UK and in certain other countries

First published 2003

British Library Cataloguing in Publication Data

Data available

Cover artwork by Joe Wright

Teacher's Notes: ISBN 978-0-19-845390-1

20 19 18 17 16 15 14

Page make-up by IFA Design Ltd, Plymouth, Devon

Printed in China by Imago